SURFACES

ERIC SCHMALTZ

SURFACES

ERIC SCHMALTZ

AFTERWORD BY
JOSEPH MOSCONI

Invisible Publishing
Halifax & Picton

Text copyright © Eric Schmaltz 2018
Afterword copyright © Joseph Mosconi 2018

All rights reserved. No part of this publication may be reproduced or transmitted in any form, by any method, without the prior written consent of the publisher, except by a reviewer, who may use brief excerpts in a review, or in the case of photocopying in Canada, a license from Access Copyright.

Library and Archives Canada Cataloguing in Publication

Schmaltz, Eric, 1988-, author
    Surfaces / Eric Schmaltz.

Poems.
Issued in print and electronic formats.
ISBN 978-1-988784-05-2 (softcover) | ISBN 978-1-988784-08-3 (EPUB)

    I. Title.

PS8637.C44912S87 2018   C811'.6   C2018-901095-9
                                                                                                                                          C2018-901096-7

Edited by Divya Victor
Cover and interior design by Megan Fildes | Typeset in Laurentian
With thanks to type designer Rod McDonald

Printed and bound in Canada
Invisible Publishing | Halifax & Picton
www.invisiblepublishing.com

We acknowledge the support of the Canada Council for the Arts, which last year invested $20.1 million in writing and publishing throughout Canada.

Canada Council Conseil des Arts
for the Arts   du Canada

"a border that feels"
— SARA AHMED, *STRANGE ENCOUNTERS*

Catalogue of Stimulations

1.1 Encounters: Schematics

2.0 Path Dependency

3.0 Substrates

1.2 Encounters: Structures

4.0 Babble

1.3 Encounters: Surfaces

5.0 Assembly Line

6.0 Interference Patterns

7.0 Afterword by Joseph Mosconi

1.1 Encounters: Schematics

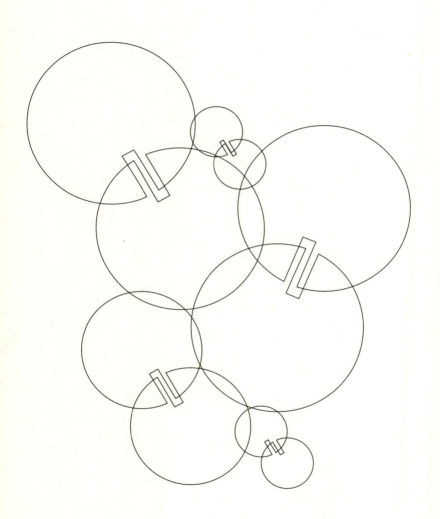

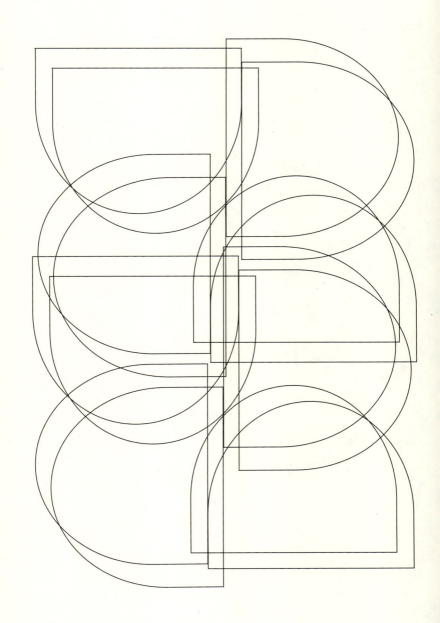

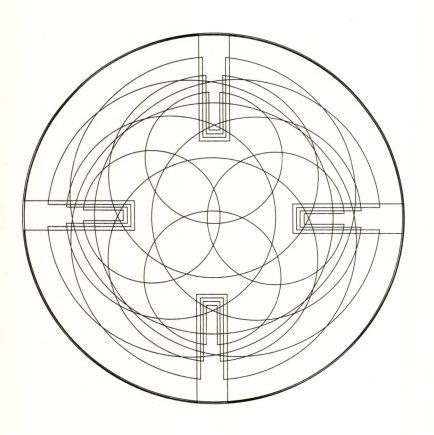

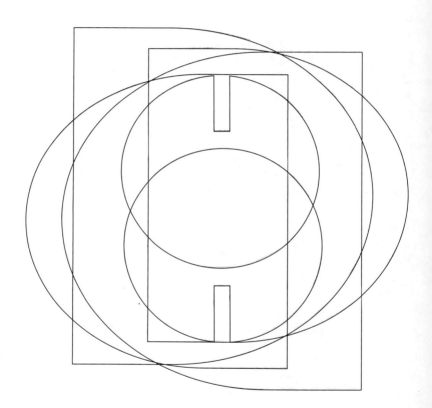

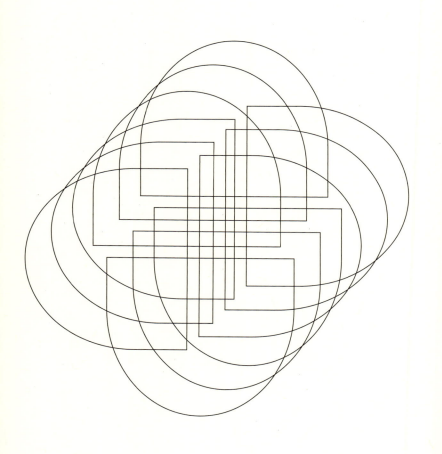

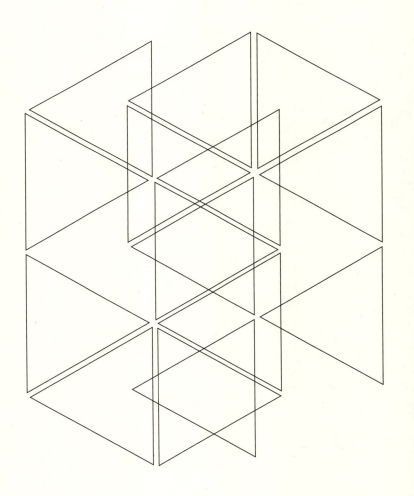

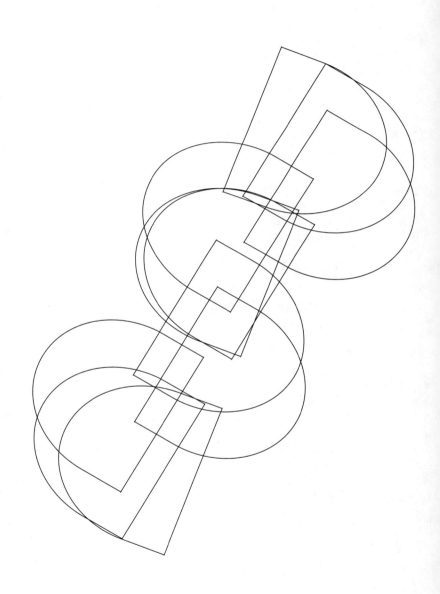

2.0 Path Dependency

"Typists connected to QWERTY alphabets, bodies shaped by the motion of the keys, one hundred words a minute, viral speed."

— Sadie Plant, *Zeros + Ones*

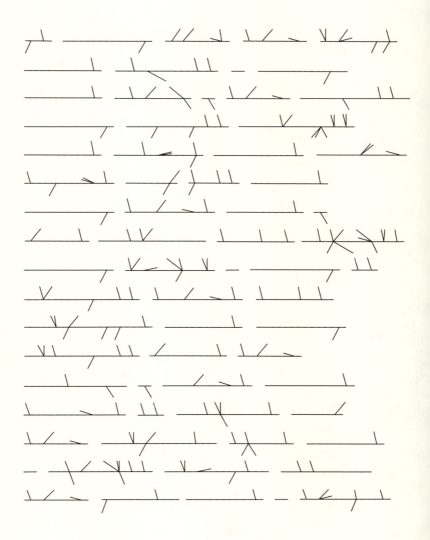

3.0 Substrates

"It was a small step to think of information as a kind of bodiless fluid that could flow between different substrates without loss of meaning or form."

– N. Katherine Hayles,
How We Became Posthuman

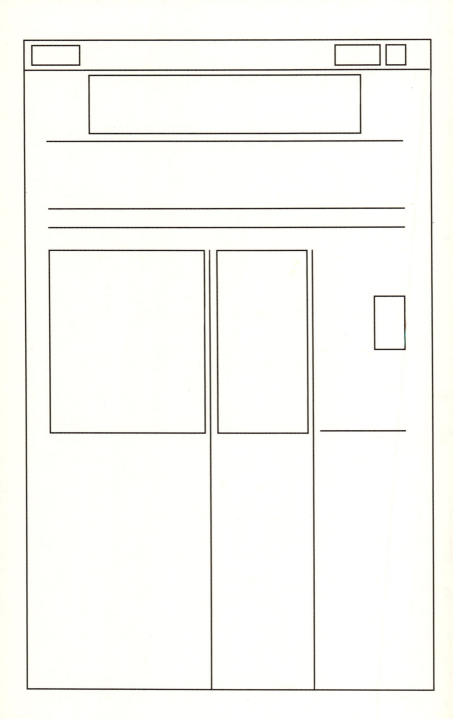

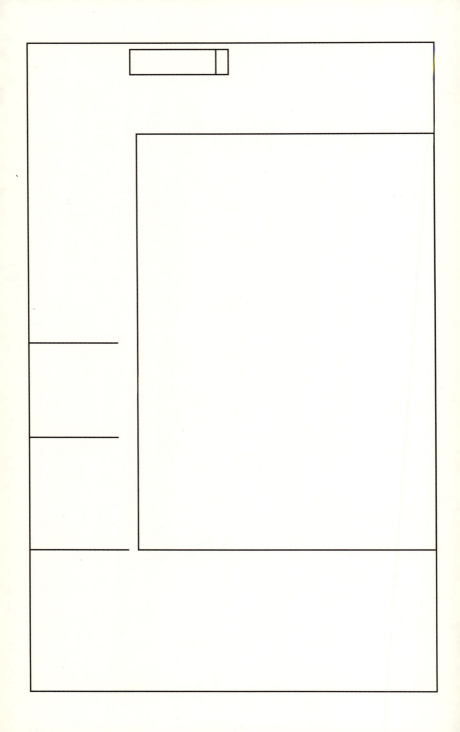

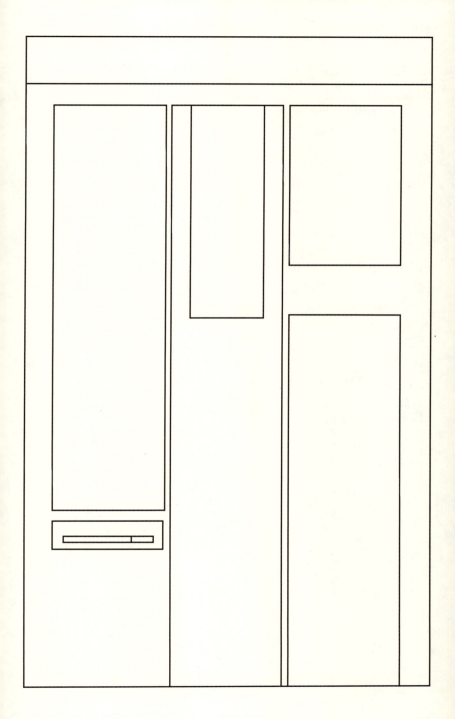

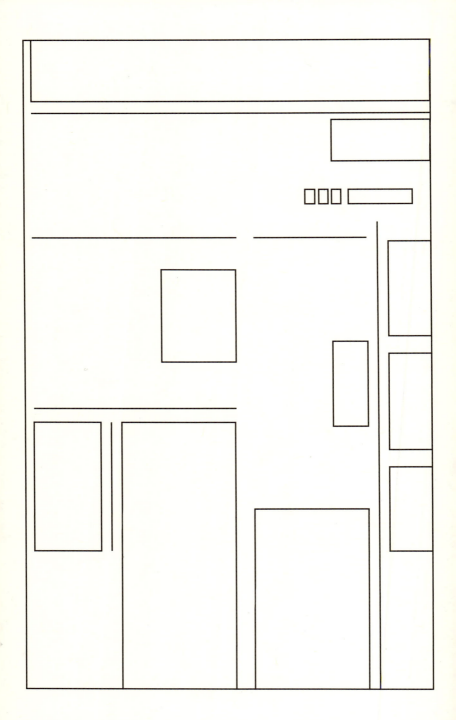

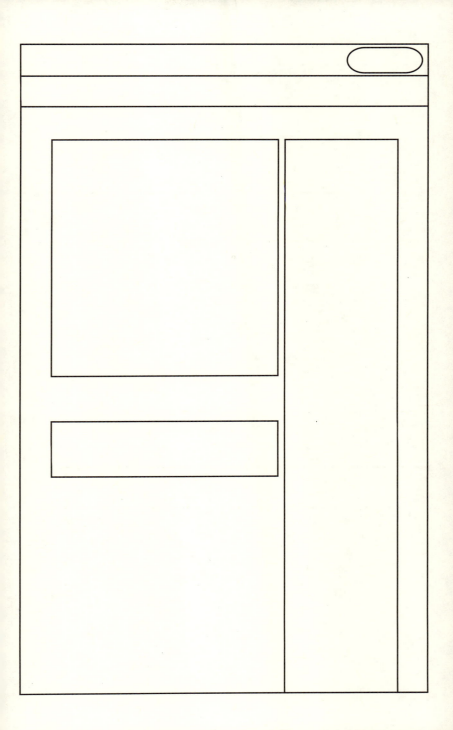

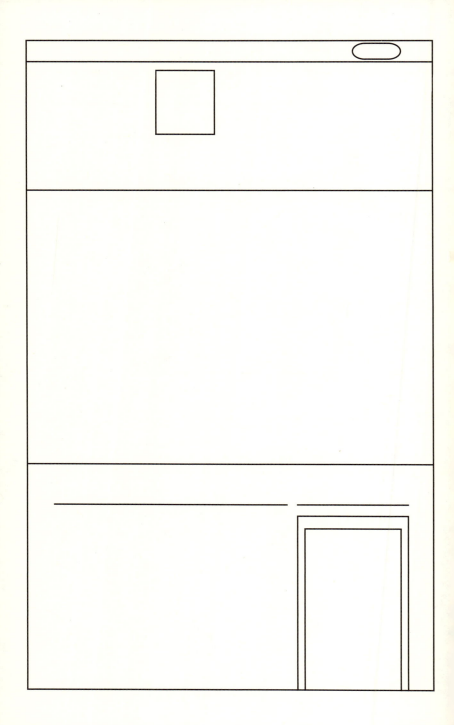

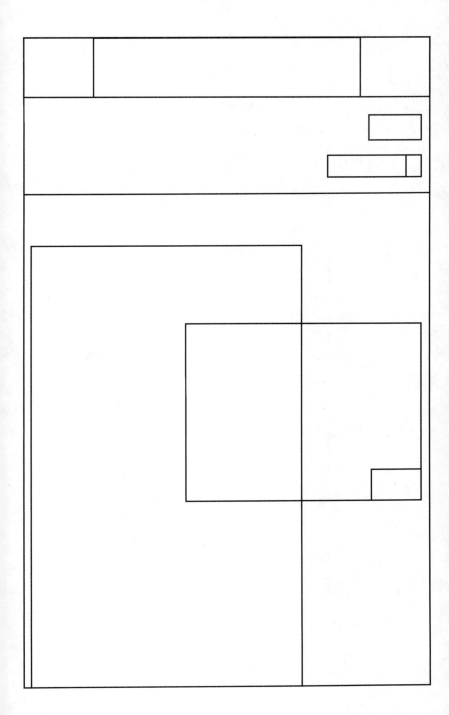

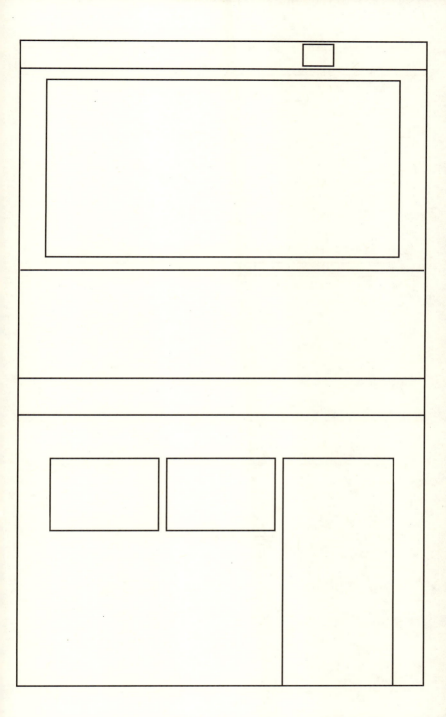

1.2 Encounters: Structures

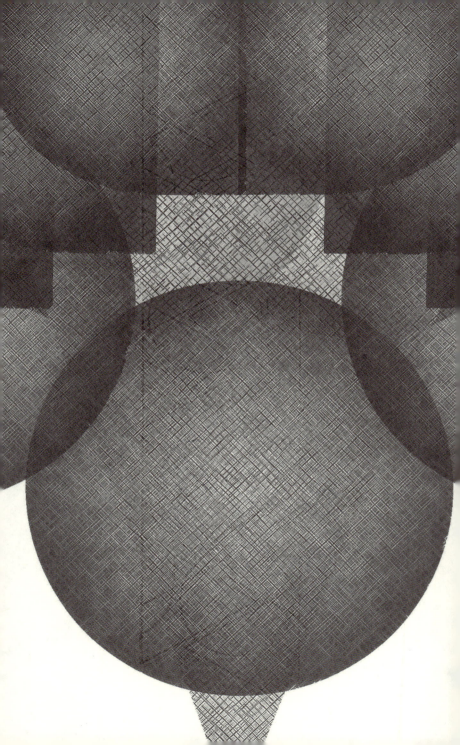

4.0 Babble

(after Joseph Mosconi)

(after Steven Shearer)

HIGH-IMPACT MONOCHROMATIC SPEED
PROFESSIONAL BLACK STAR DENSITY
WIRED INTERFACE WEIGHT CLOUD
FULL-CAPACITY PIXMA ENERGY
BIT ENABLED DIMENSIONS NETWORK
SECURE EXECUTIVE EXPRESSION
INSTANT WIRELESS JETINTELLIGENCE
INTUITIVE DEEP SPEED MEDIA
FRIENDLY DIGITAL MEMORY CONTROL
HI-CONNECTIVITY PERFORMANCE INK

GLOSSY FULL FRONTAL POLYMER
ADDITIONAL TURBO QUAD RESPONSE
SPACIOUS GIGABIT EXPERIENCE
VIRUTAL FINGERPRINT ASSEMBLY
SOLID-STATE BILINGUAL CIRCLES
ANTI-VISUAL BANDWIDTH PLATFORM
PROTECTED ION SYNC ENCLOSURE
SHARED LIGHT MEMORY BOOST
TURBO INERTIAL RETINA GRAPHICS
UNIBODY DARK DATA PROCESSOR

WATER-BASED AWARENESS DESIGN
EXTRA PATENTED PERSONALITY LINES
BALANCED G-TEC POLYMER RAZOR
VIBRANT TACTICAL ACCENT FORMULA
TRIANGULAR SILVERY LIQUID
VIBRANT BIO-POLYMER JETSTREAM
COMFORTABLE SOFT METAL DATA
ASSEMBLED ZERO GRAVITY CULTURE
QUICK-DRYING MILITARY PERSONALITY
MATERIAL INFORMATION BLEED

ULTRA PANORAMIC GRADATIONS
AUTOMATIC GRAYSCALE INTERFACE
OPTIMUM TONAL LIGHT DESIGN
INTERNAL DUAL SYSTEM DISTORTION
MULTIPAGE CATHODE SHADOW TOOLS
SUPER PIXELLATED MECURY CLOUD
OVERSIZED TIME CAPTURE UPLOAD
VIVID ARCHIVE SPACE ANALYSIS
ENHANCED VERTICAL CONSUMPTION
PRECISELY ENGINEERED ZERO

SLEEK ROTATING MECHANISM ZONE
LUXIOURIOUS RUBBER MESH BODY
VIVID METALLIC SHATTER PATTERN
PRECISION HI-POLYMER SHIMMERS
SOPHISTICATED MECHANICAL TWIST
SHOCK TECHNOLOGY EXPERIENCE
FULL-METAL ABSORPING MAXIMIZER
STUNNING AERODYNAMIC LATEX GRIP
AUTOMATIC DUAL-ACTION SPLINTER
RAPID TEXTURED DARK SYSTEM

THICKLY CRAFTED SUBLIMINAL GRIP
SUPERIOR MATTE MESSAGES
INNOVATIVE MICROBIAL DREAMS
HARDENED BACTERIA EXTENSIONS
SUPERIOR STAIN-CAUSING GRAPHITE
LARGE SOFTCORE VISUALIZATIONS
PERFECT REFORESTED CORRECTIONS
FINE HEXAGONAL SELF-EXPRESSION
SOFT TOUCH BREAK POINTS
SIMPLY WELL-DISGUISED WOOD

COLOR FEELING SELECTOR

DESIGNED CORRECTION LINE

PROFESSIONAL WORKING ERROR

INTERCHANGEABLE SHAPE INSERTION

BOLD ROYAL MARGIN CENTERING

MANUAL RETRO INK CLACK

DESIRED PAPER SPEED YIELD

AUTOMATIC LOCATION CONVERSATION

CORRECTABLE ERASABLE EPOCH

AUTOMATED CLICKING CRAFT

AMBIENT AFFECT ACCELEROMETER
ADVANCED WORD ENTERTAINMENT
DISMSISSED PREDICTION DISPLAY
IMMERSIVE PLEASURE RECOGNITION
HYBRID FINGERPRINT CORRECTION
CONVENIENT DETAILED RISK
BORDERLESS CONTROL ORGANIZATIONS
DYNAMIC PIXEL LIFE ACCESS CAPACITY
WIRELESS PERFORMANCE ENHANCER
BLUE SYNCHRONIZATION DYNAMIC

EFFORTLESS BLACK CLOUD VERSATILITY
MULTILINGUAL PIXEL PHILOSOPHY
POLARIZING POLYMER FEEL NETWORK
ELEGANT MEMORY SECURITY
EXPANDABLE INBOX LIFE LEATHER
CERTIFIED OCTA DOCUMENT BAND
NUVISION ENTERTAINMENT TEXT
ALL POLYMER ACCELEROMETER
LOUD UNLIMITED LOLLIPOP
SENSITIVE AMBIENT LANGUAGE USER

1.3 Encounters: Surfaces

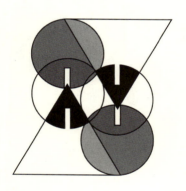

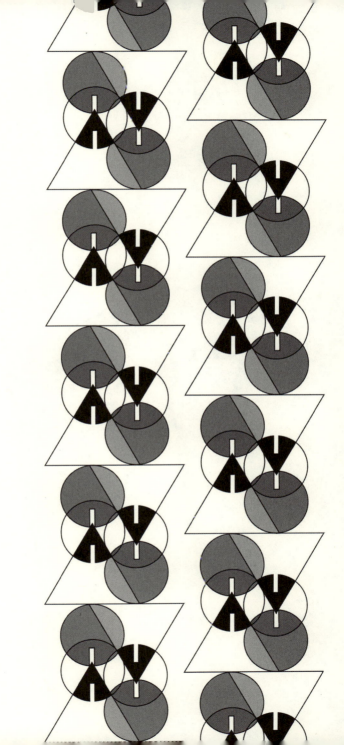

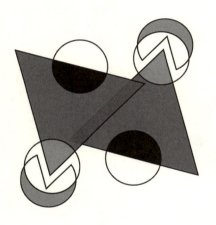

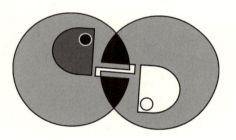

5.0 Assembly Line

"The semiotic assembly line not only produces knowledge and information but also attitudes, stereotypes of behavior, and submission to hierarchies."

— Maurizio Lazzarato, *Signs and Machines*

1

S⇐E⇐MB⇢L↓A⇢NC⇐E⇐

2

SLMCƎЛI | | |
x1 x1 x1 x1 x1 x1 x1 x4 x4 x2 x1

3

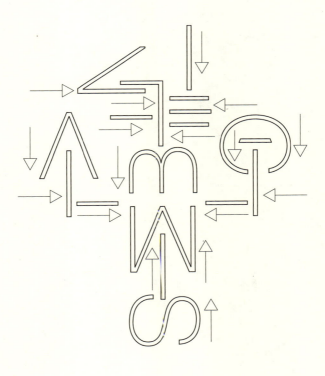

1

FEELING

2

G L N I | | |
x1 x1 x1 x5 x4 x3 x1

3

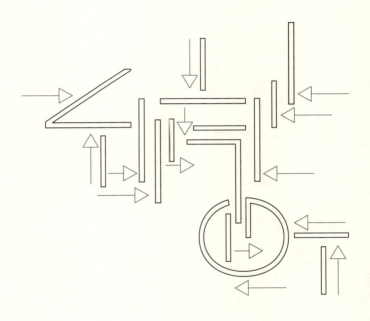

1

INFORMATION

2

 x1   x2   x1   x1   x2   x5 x1 x1 x1 x1 x1

3

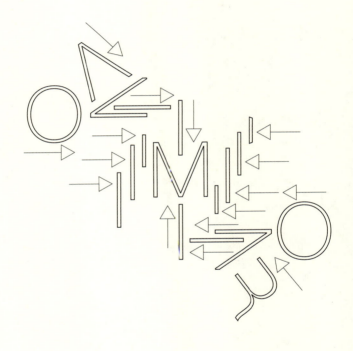

1

EMBODIMENT

2

x2　x1　x1　x1　x1　x6　x1　x1　x4　x2

3

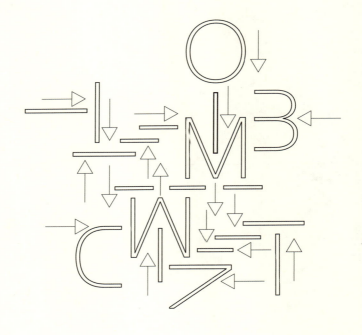

1

COMMUNICATION

2

MOCUANIII

x2 x2 x2 x1 x1 x2 x4 x1 x1 x1

3

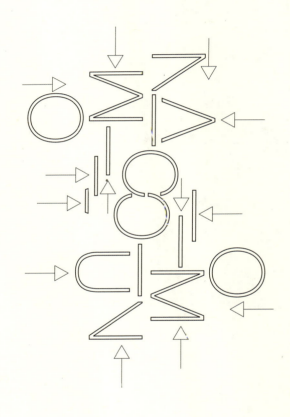

6.0 Interference Patterns

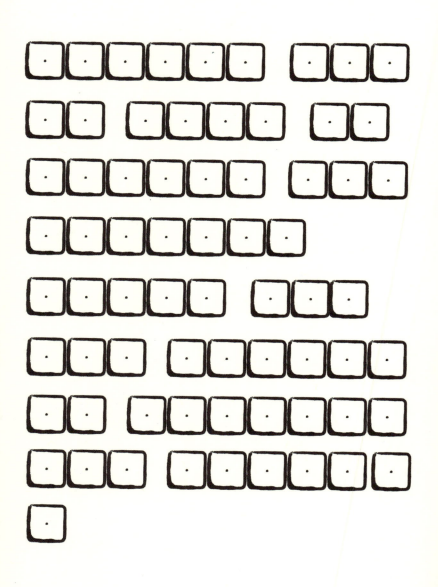

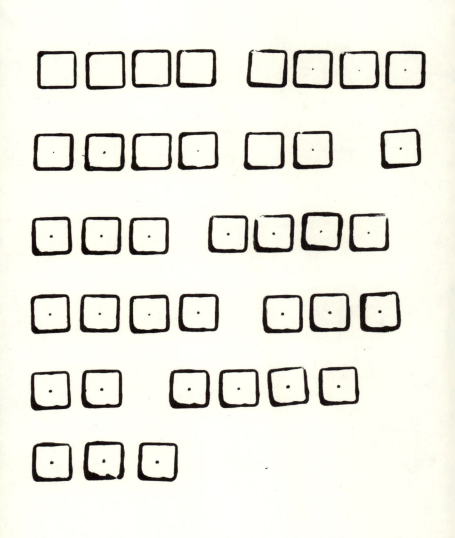

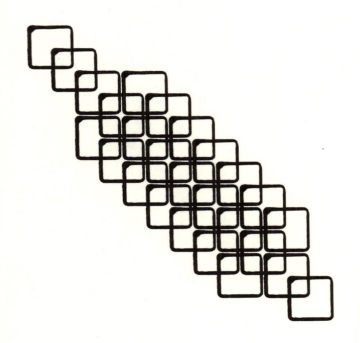

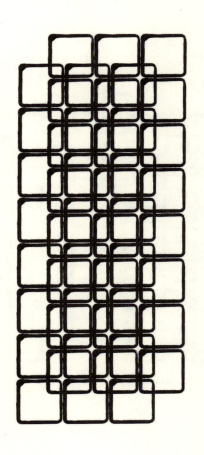

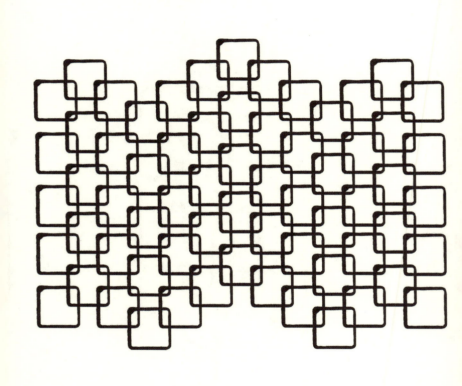

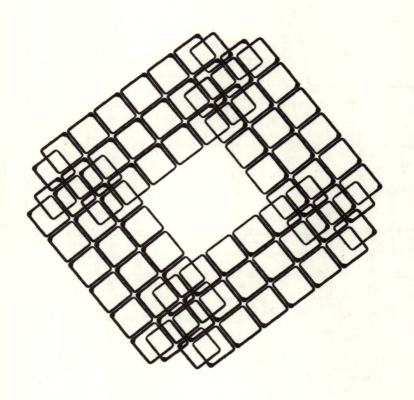

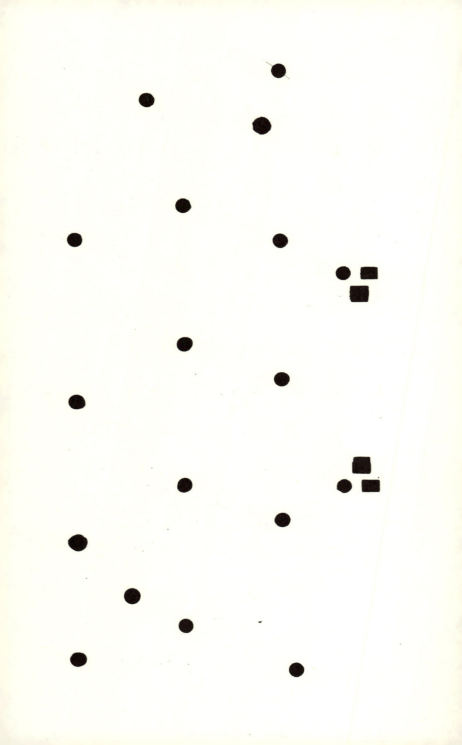

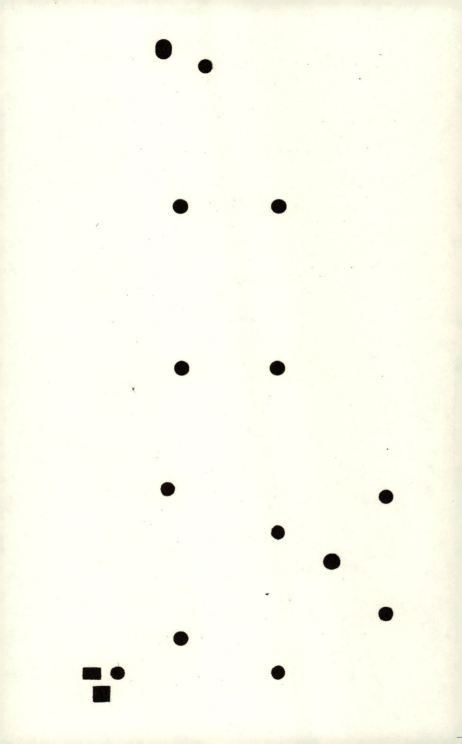

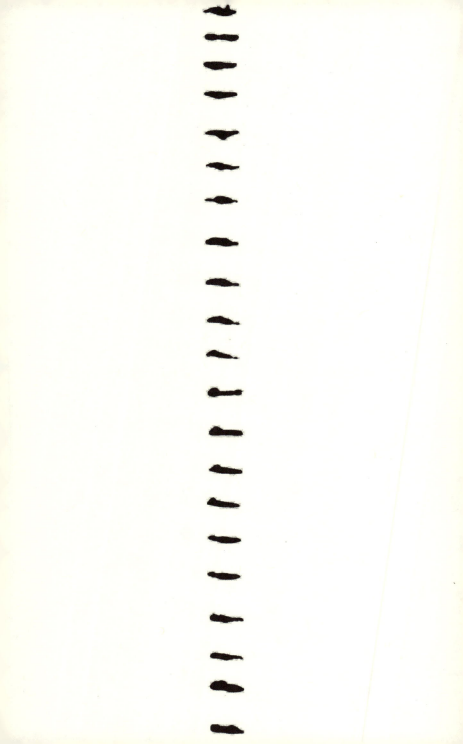

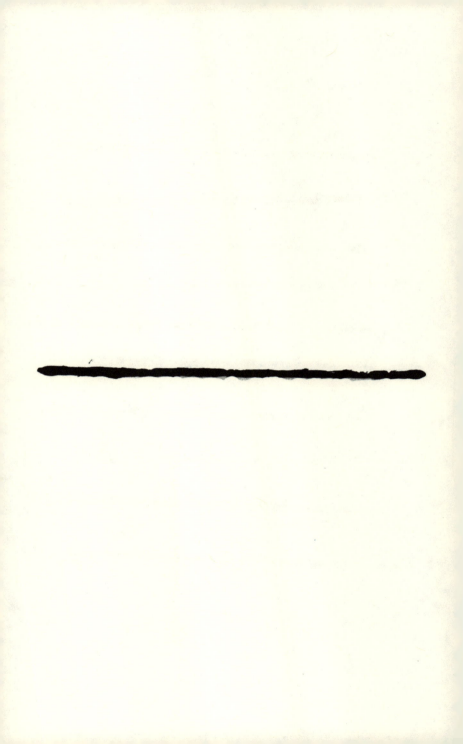

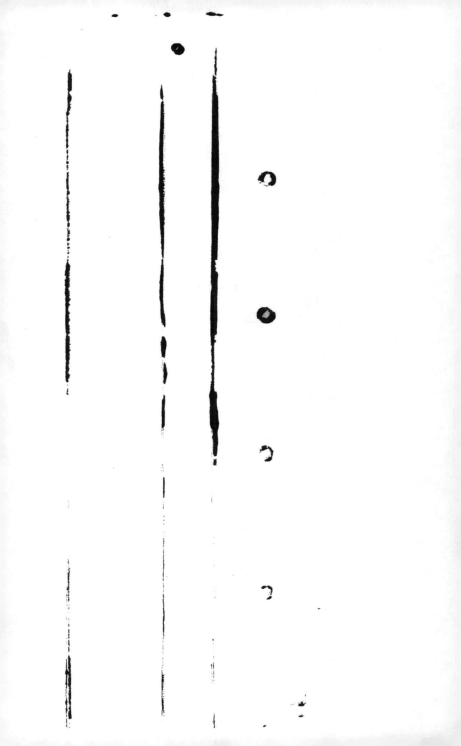

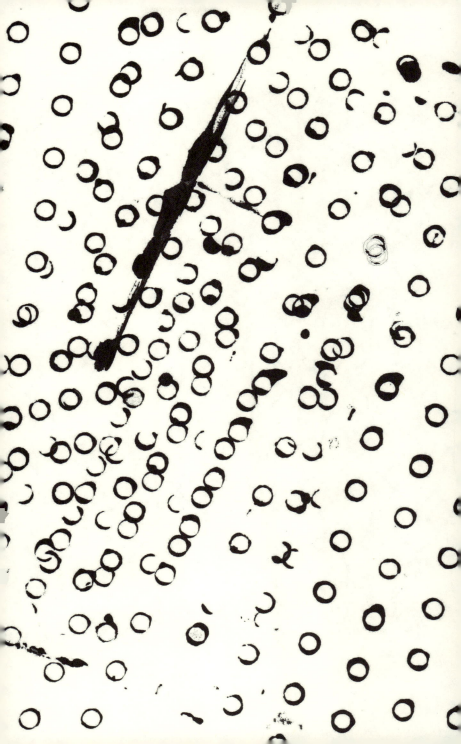

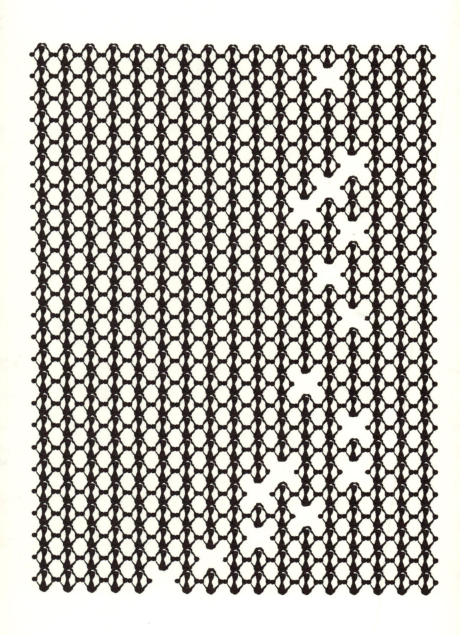

Afterword by Joseph Mosconi

THREE SUPERFICIAL THOUGHTS ON *SURFACES*

1.

There's an old one-liner, originating debatably in Aesop's Fables, that goes something like: "A glib talker has lots of depth on the surface, but deep down is pretty shallow." We won't mention again this imaginary person, this foolish wordsmith. After all, it might be me. The joke was told to me by my freshman dorm-mate in college, a smart young man named Marcus who also happened to be a punk rocker, the son of a pharmaceutical magnate, and a junky. We were debating the stylistic differences between Corinthian, Ionic, and Doric columns (I know, I know), and I undoubtedly said something incredibly pretentious and half made-up before he spat out that zinger. It has stayed with me across the decades because of its improbability: what kind of eighteen-year-old uses the word glib? The sentence was structured so oddly, and was uttered so effortlessly, that I was sure he must have memorized it and stored it carefully, ready to be weaponized against unsuspecting student combatants who make stupid arguments.

The joke is straightforward but still confounding. With its surface depths and shallow interiors, it's almost a verbal version of Wittgenstein's duck-rabbit illusion, or those abstract optical design prints that become three dimensional words or animals when you stare at them long enough. And yeah, it's also insulting.

These questions of surface and depth, of superficiality and profundity, have been a central concern of textual scholarship in the wake of Sharon Marcus and Stephen Best's call for what they term "surface reading"—an attention to surface as materiality, as verbal structure, or as an affective and ethical stance. Marcus and Best situate "surface reading" in opposition to the seemingly oppressive structures of "symptomatic reading," or the search for hidden textual truths typified by Freudian and Marxist literary criticism. "We take surface to mean what is evident, perceptible, apprehensible in texts," write Marcus and Best, "what is neither hidden nor hiding; what, in the geometrical sense, has length and breadth but no thickness, and therefore covers no depth. A surface is what insists on being looked at rather than what we must train ourselves to see through."

One of the remarkable things about Eric Schmaltz's *Surfaces* is that, like the put-down joke, and like the duck-rabbit illusion, the book manages to engage both the shallows and the depths. It asks its readers not only to confront its textual experiments—its schematics, patterns, substrates, and structures—but to think through the social, political, and cognitive contexts that lie beneath such surface encounters.

2.

Schmaltz dedicates section 4.0 of *Surfaces*, entitled "Babble," to both the artist Steven Shearer and the poet Joseph Mosconi (that would be me). Shearer's 2005 series *Poems*, comprised of black-and-white charcoal drawing and prints, updates the text art tradition popularized by artists like Ed Ruscha and Jenny Holzer via the language of heavy metal youth subcultures. My own 2013 book *Fright Catalog* similarly samples the lyrics of black and death metal bands—in addition to language culled from MMORPG chatrooms, eye-rolling art-world lingo, and weird fan fiction—in order to construct color-saturated minimalist poems. I end that book of mash-ups with a single straightforward phrase: "For engagement to be profound it must first be superficial."

It was something I'd heard the artist Thomas Hirschhorn say at a lecture in Los Angeles in 2006. That same year, his exhibition Superficial Engagement opened at the Gladstone Gallery in New York City. The installation was typical of Hirschhorn's mid-aughts output: spectacular and grim, confrontational and flimsy, with cut-rate materials, spikey mannequins, magazine clippings, and graphic photos of War on Terror victims collaged seemingly at random along several immersive display stages.

More compelling, perhaps, is Hirschhorn's press release for the show, which acts as a mini-manifesto for his provocative style. "Superficial engagement," like Marcus and Best's "surface reading," is here envisioned as a political, ethical, and aesthetic position—as well as a challenge to the viewer and reader. "Superficiality is not negative," writes Hirschhorn. "Superficiality is the condition for a real engagement because if there is no engagement on the surface, there cannot be a profound engagement. To go deeply into something, I must at first begin with its surface."

"Babble" superficially resembles certain aspects of both *Poems* and *Fright Catalog*, but what is so brilliant about the poem sequence (if one can call it that) is precisely Schmaltz's superficial engagement with both the work of his predecessors and his own source material. Instead of appropriating the language produced by abject youth subcultures, Schmaltz examines "the very technical and physical language used to advertise writing, reading, and printing devices" and manages to render this commercial language as frightening as the most repulsive and foul death metal lyric. From "PROFESSIONAL BLACK STAR DENSITY" to "POLARIZING POLYMER FEEL NETWORK," the poem traces the history of writing instruments from a supposedly deep language-centered era to what Gavin Mueller calls, in a recent essay, "the depthlessness of image-based culture."

3.

In an interview, the late artist Mike Kelley claimed that what he disliked about a lot of contemporary artists is that they are not willing to be fools, to put themselves on the line in some shared emotional way. As I contemplated this, I received an obscure, almost clairvoyant impression that Eric Schmaltz's *Surfaces* has a very clever premise. It is Edgar Allan Poe's "The Purloined Letter" rewritten. A letter has gone missing. It has in fact been stolen. We do not know its contents. We do know that its contents contain compromising information that could be damaging to a person of high importance. Blackmail ensues. The police, despite their best efforts, can find no trace of the letter. They have looked deep. They have searched the home of the alleged thief. They have searched the body of the alleged thief. They believe the thief to be a fool. Well, "not altogether a fool," say the police. "But then he's a poet, which I take to be only one remove from a fool." There is an assumption that the thief is a fool because he is a poet. There is an assumption that the poet must always signify depth. There is an assumption that the letter must be hidden somewhere deep. There is an assumption, ultimately, that a fool is a bad thing to be. I do not wish to be insulting, but I have come to believe that the superficial and the foolish, following Hirschhorn and Kelley, are in no way negative, but rather the conditions for real engagement and critique. They are the very line that provides shared emotion—or, as Schmaltz indicates in his book's epigraph by Sara Ahmed, "a border that feels." In the end, Poe's hero detective C. Augustine Dupin discovers the stolen letter hidden in plain sight—right on the surface of things, one could say.

Notes

All sections of "Encounters" are composed using only the geometric shapes that make up the closed parts of letters A, B, D, O, P, Q, and R. The shape made by the enclosure of a letter is referred to as a "counter" in typography. When developing this series, I considered the implications of the article "Phantoms Limbs and Neural Plasticity" (2000) by Vilayanur S. Ramachandran and Diane Rogers-Ramachandran, from whom I've learned about the brain's shocking capacities to reinterpret body image. Thank you to Divya Victor for pointing me toward this article.

"Path Dependency" is a translation of a short article that I wrote for rob mclennan's "On Writing" series. In "Path Dependency," I translate each word of the source text into a visual representation of finger movements across the keyboard, away from home row, as they produce letters on the digital page. This piece explores digital culture and embodiment or what N. Katherine Hayles refers to as the idea of a "bodiless fluid" during the Information Age.

Each panel in "Babble" is composed around the very technical and physical language used to advertise writing, reading, and printing devices including the wooden pencil, pen, mechanical pencil, typewriter, scanner, printer, laptop, tablet, and smart phone. The language is sourced from Amazon entries, cut up using an online cut-up application on languageisavirus.com, and then recomposed in the present form.

Each panel in "Substrates" is composed by tracing the webpage templates used by select news and literature websites frequented by the author. Websites traced in this section include *New York Times*, *Jacket2*, *Poetry Foundation*, *Lemon Hound*, *Book Forum*, *Los Angeles Review of Books*, *Chicago*

Review of Books, *Boston Review*, *4Columns*, and *The Globe and Mail* book section. Excerpts from this series were published by No Press.

"Assembly Line" is composed by deconstructing and reconstructing the lines of each letter of the source words. This section adapts the aesthetic of the Ikea instruction manual as an investigation into language's visuality and permutability alongside side ideas related to Ikea-hacking and play.

Inspired by *The Plastic Typewriter* by Paul Dutton, "Interference Patterns" is composed by using a dismantled keyboard, black paint, white cardstock, and a digital scanner. It should be noted that the epigraph of the chapbook version of this series (published by above/ground press) is framed as an excerpt from Dutton's text. Those words, also used by Dutton, were borrowed from a gospel song entitled "Certainly Lord."

Acknowledgements

First, infinite thanks to my editor Divya Victor for traversing these surfaces to their depths. Without your perception, your poetic sensibility, your time, and your knowledge, this book would have not been assembled. I will remember your kindness and generosity.

Without Leigh Nash and the team at Invisible Publishing, this book would never have materialized. Thank you, Leigh, for your time, energy, and resources. Thank you for taking a risk with this book, and committing yourself as a publisher to emergent voices and alternative modes. Thank you, too, Andrew Faulkner for making first contact, for encouraging me to fulfill the schematics. Thank you to Julie Wilson for coordinating and to Megan Fildes for her outstanding design.

My thanks to the editors who set forth sections and/or versions from *Surfaces* in periodicals and chapbooks before they were published here: derek beaulieu for No Press, Michael e. Casteels for *Illiterature*, Amanda Earl for *Brick Books*, Karen Correia da Silva, Anna Veprinska, Neal Armstrong for *Steel Bananas*, Chris Johnson and others for *Arc Poetry Magazine*, rob mclennan for above/ground press and *Touch the Donkey*, Michael Nardone for *Amodern*, Anthony Opal for *The Economy*, and Catherine Parayre for *ti<*.

Sincere gratitude to curators and organizers for giving versions of these works an opportunity to come off the page: the collective at the Sugar City Arts Collective (Buffalo), David Hamilton at LAB T.O. (Toronto), Catherine Parayre for Rodman Hall (St. Catharines), Natasha Pedros and Stephen Remus at Niagara Artists Centre (St. Catharines), Stephen Trothen and Marcel O'Gorman for the Critical

Media Lab (Kitchener), and Daniel Zomparelli for Havana Gallery (Vancouver).

Thank you derek beaulieu, Amaranth Borsuk, Donato Mancini, and Divya Victor for the kind and supportive words that accompany this book into the world. Your multifaceted work motivates, inspires, and humbles me. Likewise, Joseph Mosconi, thank you for your generous critical spirit and for providing scaffolding for the book. It means so much to me to be moving in sync with all of you for now.

I am so truly grateful for the friendships, mentorships, and various forms of friendly assistance I've had over the years of composing this book. Thank you to the following people for conversing, critiquing, and supporting in your various ways: Barsin Aghajan, Gary Barwin, Caleb Beckwith, Gregory Betts, Lindsay Cahill, Stephen Cain, MLA Chernoff, Marc Couroux, Paul Dutton, Geof Huth, Joseph Ianni, Aaron Kreuter, Mat Laporte, rob mclennan, Phil Miletic, Julia Polyck-O'Neill, Kate Siklosi, Kasia Smuga, Dani Spinosa, and Andy Weaver.

Finally, thank you, Alysha Dawn, for showing me what is possible.

INVISIBLE PUBLISHING produces fine Canadian literature for those who enjoy such things. As a not-for-proft publisher, our work includes building communities that sustain and encourage engaging, literary, and current writing.

Invisible Publishing has been in operation for over a decade. We released our first fiction titles in the spring of 2007, and our catalogue has come to include works of graphic fiction and non-fiction, pop culture biographies, experimental poetry, and prose.

We are committed to publishing diverse voices and experiences. In acknowledging historical and systemic barriers, and the limits of our existing catalogue, we strongly encourage LGBTQ2SIA+, Indigenous, and writers of colour to submit their work.

Invisible Publishing is also home to the Bibliophonic series of music books and the Throwback series of CanLit reissues.

If you'd like to know more please get in touch:
info@invisiblepublishing.com